Heroes to the Rescue

Written by Esther Ripley

DK | Penguin Random House

Editor Beth Davies
Designer Stefan Georgiou
Pre-Production Producer Siu Yin Chan
Producer Louise Daly
Managing Editor Paula Regan
Managing Art Editor Guy Harvey
Art Director Lisa Lanzarini
Publisher Julie Ferris
Publishing Director Simon Beecroft

Designed for DK by Rich T Media

Reading Consultant Linda Gambrell, PhD.

Dorling Kindersley would like to thank Randi Sørensen,
Paul Hansford, and Martin Leighton Lindhardt at the LEGO Group.

First American Edition, 2016
Published in the United States by DK Publishing
345 Hudson Street, New York, New York 10014

ISBN 978-1-4654-5190-3 (Hardback)
ISBN 978-1-4654-5189-7 (Paperback)

DK books are available at special discounts when purchased in bulk for sales promotions,
premiums, fund-raising, or educational use. For details, contact: DK Publishing Special
Markets, 345 Hudson Street, New York, New York 10014
SpecialSales@dk.com

Printed and bound in China

www.LEGO.com
www.dk.com

A WORLD OF IDEAS:
SEE ALL THERE IS TO KNOW

2

Contents

Welcome to the City

The streets of LEGO® City are busy with cars, trucks, bikes, and people. The emergency services are always on patrol to help any citizens who are in trouble.

A police car controls the traffic in the main square. Firefighters rush to the scene of a fire. Their fire engine has all the equipment that they need to put out the blaze.

At the Station

When there is a fire emergency,
the Fire Chief takes the call.
He rings the alarm to alert
the firefighters, who are ready
to spring into action.
Brrrring! Brrrring!

When the firefighters hear
the alarm, they gather their
equipment and push open the
fire station door. The crew is
ready to go!

INSIDE THE
FIRE STATION

Down at the station, the firefighters keep their equipment in tip-top condition. They need to have everything ready in case of an emergency.

The satellite dish receives calls for help.

The pole is the fastest way to the ground.

A tool rack keeps equipment neat and tidy.

The station's dog is an important part of the team.

Fire symbol identifies the building.

The helicopter sits on the landing pad.

Tired firefighters can rest in the bunk beds.

The garage bay doors roll up and down.

Rotating doors provide a quick exit route.

Fire!

Oh no! The lighthouse lamp has overheated and burst into flames. The lighthouse keeper is scared, but he knows just who to call!

The fire rescue boat is soon speeding across the water to put out the fire.

Save the Day

The fire rescue boat is full of tools that the firefighters need to save the lighthouse. A water cannon on a long crane will easily reach the top of the lighthouse.

One firefighter controls the water cannon and aims a jet of water at the fire. A trained diver gets ready to rescue the lighthouse keeper if he falls into the ocean.

FIREFIGHTING VEHICLES

The LEGO® City firefighters deal with all kinds of emergencies. Their vehicles get them to the action on land, on water, and even up in the air.

FIRE ENGINE

FEATURES: Fire hoses, warning lights, ladder
SPECIALTY: The big engine gets to the fire fast. The firefighters use the ladder to reach the blaze or to save people who are trapped.

MOTORCYCLE

FEATURES: Blue flashing light, powerful engine
SPECIALTY: A firefighter on a bike can get to an emergency even quicker than the fire engine.

HELICOPTER

FEATURES: Spinning rotors, on-board equipment and hoses
SPECIALTY: The fire helicopter puts out fires in places that are hard to reach.

RESCUE BOAT

FEATURES: Water cannons, satellite dish, rescue dinghies
SPECIALTY: The fire boat is used for emergencies on water. It rescues people trapped on boats and lighthouses.

CHIEF'S CAR

FEATURES: Warning lights, big wheels
SPECIALTY: The Fire Chief uses his car to get to the emergency fast. He organizes the crew at the scene.

UTILITY TRUCK

FEATURES: Boxes and racks of equipment, side-opening door
SPECIALTY: This sturdy truck carries axes, oxygen tanks, and fire extinguishers.

Motorcycle Emergency

Ouch! A motorcycle rider has skidded on the wet road and fallen off his bike. Two kind citizens jump out of their van and run to help him.

They call for an ambulance to take the injured rider to the hospital.

The motorcycle rider must not move in case he has broken any bones.

Airplane Rescue

The air ambulance plane rescues injured people from places that are difficult to reach.

It can deliver people to the hospital much faster than an ordinary ambulance can.

The paramedics carry patients on board using a stretcher. They are trained to treat patients on the move and even save their lives.

Police

LEGO® City is kept safe by its brave police force. When a citizen is lost or in trouble, the police officers on the streets are there to help out.

POLICE LINE—DO NOT CROSS

The police keep the traffic
moving and catch crooks.
They have high-speed cars
and motorcycles to get them
to the scene of an accident
or a robbery.

POLICE LINE—DO NOT CROSS

LEGO® CITY POLICE
MOST WANTED

Crooks are always up to no good in LEGO® City. Keep an eye out for these bad guys. The police need your help to track them down.

ROBBER

This wicked crook has stolen loads of loot.

WANTED FOR: Raids on three banks.
SKILLS: Safe cracker, has a fast getaway car.

GRAFFITIST

This pesky artist paints everywhere he goes.
WANTED FOR: Spraying walls with messy paint.
SKILLS: Good climber, not afraid of heights, works fast.

SHOPLIFTER

No store is safe from this crook.

WANTED FOR: Stealing candy, soda, and toys.
SKILLS: Has many disguises, wears a coat with deep pockets.

VANDAL

This silly vandal causes lots of damage at night.

WANTED FOR: Kicking holes in garden fences and smashing windows.
SKILLS: Fast runner, very strong.

PICKPOCKET

Citizens should beware of this crook.

WANTED FOR: Stealing wallets, purses, and phones.
SKILLS: Light fingers, disappears fast when the police appear.

JEWEL THIEF

This thief can't resist gold and diamonds.

WANTED FOR: Burglary in the Jewelry Store and City Museum.
SKILLS: Picking locks, opening high windows.

Prison Island

The crooks who make trouble in LEGO® City are locked up in cells on Prison Island. Prison Island is a fortress with bars on the windows and powerful searchlights. The police officers keep watch day and night.

The crooks are pretending to rest in their cells. But they have a sneaky plan to escape from the prison!

HIGH SECURITY ON
PRISON ISLAND

Nothing is left to chance on Prison Island. The police helicopter is on patrol. The guards keep watch with their searchlights and radios.

The helicopter transports crooks to the island.

The prison is built on a rocky island base.

The bright landing pad stands out from the gray rocks.

A satellite dish keeps contact with the mainland.

The watchtower has windows on every side.

Security cameras film prisoners day and night.

POLICE

A basement pipe has been left open!

Escape

Sound the alarm! The crooks have escaped from their cells on Prison Island.

Oh no! Two prisoners are speeding away in an inflatable boat. Look up at the sky! Two more crooks are floating away in a hot-air balloon. The guards call for help to catch the sneaky crooks.

Crooks' Hideout

The crooks have built a secret hideout on a rock in the middle of the ocean.

They have lots of tools and stolen objects—including a safe full of money!

The crooks think no one will find them here. They hope the police do not come looking for them.

Inside their hideout the crooks can relax. They have even stolen a coffee machine so they can make themselves a hot drink!

On the Lookout

The police are on the lookout for the escaped prisoners. Police cars race through the city streets. The police look for clues about where the crooks are hiding.

Whirring across the sky, the police helicopter has a bird's-eye view of the city and the ocean. The pilot uses his radio to tell the other officers where the crooks might be hiding.

I SPY CROOKS

Watch out crooks! A police helicopter has spotted the crooks' island hideout. He radios his fellow police officers.

Captured!

The officers on the police
boat use their satellite dish
to find the crooks' lair. There
is nowhere for the crooks to hide!

A police officer arrests the crooks. He puts handcuffs on one prisoner and marches the pair onto the boat. The police boat captain takes them all back to Prison Island.

LEGO® CITY NEWS

FIRE AT SEA

The LEGO® City fire rescue boat carried out a daring operation yesterday when a lighthouse caught fire. Firefighters soon put out the flames and rescued the keeper in a dinghy.

BIKER IN TROUBLE

Paramedics raced to a motorcycle accident in LEGO City on Saturday. The biker was taken to the hospital with a broken leg.

Continued inside

PRISON BREAKOUT

There was a surprise breakout from Prison Island this week. Police boats, helicopters, and cars soon tracked down the escaped prisoners.

Continued inside

"Your city is in safe hands."

LEGO City Police Chief

Quiz

1. Who rings the alarm to wake up the firefighters?

2. What animal works at the fire station?

3. What building bursts into flames?

4. What color is the flashing light on the Fire Motorcycle?

5. What type of vehicle does the Fire Chief use?

6. Who needs rescuing by the air ambulance plane?

7. Where does the motorcycle accident take place?

8. Which crook smashes windows?

9. True or False: The Jewel Thief robbed a millionaire's mansion.

10. What building do the prisoners escape from?

Answers on page 45.

Glossary

Citizen
Someone who lives in a town or city

Emergency
An unplanned and dangerous situation

Equipment
Items needed for a certain task

Inflatable
Able to be filled with air

Injured
Hurt or wounded

Fire extinguisher
A portable device that helps put out fires

Fortress
A building designed to stop people from getting in and out easily

Graffitist
A person who paints on walls without permission

Paramedic
A person trained to treat injured people

Pickpocket
A person who steals from other people's pockets

Satellite dish
A device that helps to send and receive messages

Searchlight
A powerful light that can be used to look for people

Stretcher
A frame used for carrying injured people

Vandal
A person who deliberately destroys other people's things

Answers to the Quiz on pages 42–43.
1. Fire Chief 2. Dog 3. Lighthouse 4. Blue 5. Car 6. Motorcycle Rider 7. Main square 8. The vandal 9. False: He robbed the Jewelry Store and the City Museum 10. Prison Island

Guide for Parents

This book is part of an exciting four-level reading series for children, developing the habit of reading widely for both pleasure and information. These chapter books have a compelling main narrative to suit your child's reading ability. Each book is designed to develop your child's reading skills, fluency, grammar awareness, and comprehension in order to build confidence and engagement when reading.

Ready for a *Level 2* book

YOUR CHILD SHOULD

- be familiar with using beginning letter sounds and context clues to figure out unfamiliar words.
- be aware of the need for a slight pause at commas and a longer one at periods.
- alter his/her expression for questions and exclamations.

A VALUABLE AND SHARED READING EXPERIENCE

For many children, reading requires much effort, but adult participation can make this both fun and easier. So here are a few tips on how to use this book with your child.

TIP 1 **Check out the contents together before your child begins:**
- read the text about the book on the back cover.
- flip through the book and stop to chat about the contents page together to heighten your child's interest and expectation.
- make use of unfamiliar or difficult words on the page in a brief discussion.
- chat about the nonfiction reading features used in the book, such as headings, captions, lists, or charts.

TIP 2 Support your child as he/she reads the story pages:

- give the book to your child to read and turn the pages.

- where necessary, encourage your child to break a word into syllables, sound out each one, and then flow the syllables together. Ask him/her to reread the sentence to check the meaning.

- when there's a question mark or an exclamation mark, encourage your child to vary his/her voice as he/she reads the sentence. Demonstrate how to do this if it is helpful.

TIP 3 Chat at the end of each page:

- ask questions about the text and the meaning of the words used. These help to develop comprehension skills and awareness of the language used.

A FEW ADDITIONAL TIPS

- Always encourage your child to try reading difficult words by themselves. Praise any self-corrections, for example, "I like the way you sounded out that word and then changed the way you said it, to make sense."

- Try to read together everyday. Little and often is best. After 10 minutes of reading, only keep going if your child wants to read on.

- Read other books of different types to your child just for enjoyment and information.

Series consultant, **Dr. Linda Gambrell**, Distinguished Professor of Education at Clemson University, has served as President of the National Reading Conference, the College Reading Association, and the International Reading Association.

Index